SUPER SIMPLE ★

PRESIDENTS' DAY

ACTIVITIES

★ FUN AND EASY HOLIDAY PROJECTS FOR KIDS ★

Megan Borgert-Spaniol

Consulting Editor, Diane Craig, M.A./Reading Specialist

Super Sandcastle

An Imprint of Abdo Publishing
abdopublishing.com

abdopublishing.com

Published by Abdo Publishing, a division of ABDO, PO Box 398166, Minneapolis, Minnesota 55439.
Copyright © 2018 by Abdo Consulting Group, Inc. International copyrights reserved in all countries.
No part of this book may be reproduced in any form without written permission from the publisher.
Super SandCastle™ is a trademark and logo of Abdo Publishing.

Printed in the United States of America, North Mankato, Minnesota

102017
012018

 THIS BOOK CONTAINS
RECYCLED MATERIALS

Design: Alison Stuerman, Mighty Media, Inc.
Production: Mighty Media, Inc.
Editor: Rebecca Felix
Cover Photographs: Mighty Media, Inc.; Shutterstock
Interior Photographs: Mighty Media, Inc.; sellke/Flickr; Shutterstock

The following manufacturers/names appearing in this book are trademarks: Craft Smart®,
Elmer's®, Elmer's® Glue-All™, Sharpie®

Publisher's Cataloging-in-Publication Data
Names: Borgert-Spaniol, Megan, author.
Title: Super simple Presidents' Day activities: fun and easy holiday projects for kids /
by Megan Borgert-Spaniol.
Other titles: Fun and easy holiday projects for kids
Description: Minneapolis, Minnesota : Abdo Publishing, 2018. | Series: Super simple holidays |
Identifiers: LCCN 2017946526 | ISBN 9781532112461 (lib.bdg.) | ISBN 9781614799887 (ebook)
Subjects: LCSH: Patriotism--United States--Juvenile literature. | Handicraft--Juvenile literature. |
    Holiday decorations--Juvenile literature.
Classification: DDC 745.5--dc23
LC record available at https://lccn.loc.gov/2017946526

Super SandCastle™ books are created by a team of professional educators, reading specialists, and content developers around five essential components—phonemic awareness, phonics, vocabulary, text comprehension, and fluency—to assist young readers as they develop reading skills and strategies and increase their general knowledge. All books are written, reviewed, and leveled for guided reading and early reading intervention for use in shared, guided, and independent reading and writing activities to support a balanced approach to literacy instruction.

TO ADULT HELPERS

The craft projects in this series are fun and simple. There are just a few things to remember to keep kids safe. Some projects require the use of sharp or hot objects or involve food items with allergy triggers. Also, kids may be using messy materials such as glue or paint. Make sure they protect their clothes and work surfaces. Review the projects before starting and be ready to assist when necessary.

KEY SYMBOLS

Watch for these warning symbols in this book. Here is what each one means.

HOT!
This project requires the use of a hot tool. Get help!

NUTS!
This project includes the use of nuts. Find out whether anyone you are serving has a nut allergy.

SHARP!
You will be working with a sharp object. Get help!

CONTENTS ★

HAPPY HOLIDAYS!

Holidays are great times to celebrate with family and friends. Many people have favorite holiday **traditions**. Some traditions are hundreds of years old. But people start new traditions too, such as making holiday foods and crafts.

PRESIDENTS' DAY

Presidents' Day is a US holiday. It began on February 22, 1885. Then, it was a celebration of first US president George Washington's birthday.

In 1971, the US government moved the celebration of Washington's birthday to the third Monday of February. People began calling the holiday Presidents' Day to include former US president Abraham Lincoln. Today, Americans celebrate Presidents' Day in honor of all the nation's presidents.

CELEBRATE PRESIDENTS' DAY

People across the United States celebrate Presidents' Day in many ways. How do you celebrate this holiday?

REENACTMENTS

On Presidents' Day, groups of actors **reenact** historical scenes. The US **Senate** has a similar **tradition**. A Senate member reads Washington's Farewell Address to a crowd each year near Presidents' Day.

HISTORY LESSONS

Many US schools teach students about the nation's presidents near Presidents' Day. George Washington and Abraham Lincoln are two of its most celebrated leaders.

GEORGE WASHINGTON

George Washington led the nation from 1789 to 1797. Before becoming president, he led the group that wrote the US **Constitution**.

ABRAHAM LINCOLN

Abraham Lincoln was the sixteenth president of the United States. He led the nation from 1861 to 1865. He fought to end slavery in the United States.

MATERIALS ★

Here are some of the materials that you will need for the projects in this book.

ALUMINUM FOIL BANANAS BLUEBERRIES BUTTONS CARD STOCK CARDBOARD

COINS COLORED PAPER COTTON BALLS CRAFT GLUE CRAFT KNIFE FOOD COLORING

GLITTER

GLUE STICK

GRAHAM CRACKERS

HOT GLUE GUN & GLUE STICKS

MARKERS

PAINT

PAINTBRUSHES

PAPER PLATES

PEANUT BUTTER

PENCILS

POTATOES

PRETZEL RODS

RIBBON

SHARP KNIFE

SHREDDED COCONUT

STRAWBERRIES

WHITE COFFEE FILTERS

WOODEN SKEWERS

9

STATELY STARS STAMP CARD

Construct your own stamp to make stars like those on the nation's flag!

1 Have an adult help you cut a potato in half crosswise.

2 Draw a star on each cut side of the potato.

3 Have an adult help you carve out the potato around each star outline. Cut enough away that the star sticks out to become a stamp.

4 Cut 1 inch (2.5 cm) off one short side and one long side of the card stock. Glue the trimmed card stock onto the center of a full sheet of blue paper. Let the glue dry.

5 Put some red and blue paint on a paper plate. Dip one stamp into red paint. Dip the other into blue paint. Stamp red and blue stars onto the card stock. Let the paint dry.

6 Fold the paper in half to make a card.

7 Write a Presidents' Day message in your card and send it to someone!

2

3

5

RED, WHITE & BLUE BUNTING

Hang painted coffee filters to celebrate Presidents' Day in a colorful way!

WHAT YOU NEED

newspaper

white coffee filters

red & blue paint

paint brushes

ribbon

scissors

glue stick or double-sided tape

12

1 Cover your work surface with newspaper. Lay one coffee filter flat. Paint a blue circle in its center. Paint the filter's border red.

2 Repeat step 1 with 10 to 15 coffee filters. Let the paint dry.

3 Lay the dried coffee filters in a row. Space them evenly with their painted sides facedown.

4 Cut a long piece of ribbon. Place it across the middle of the coffee filters.

5 Fold one coffee filter in half over the ribbon so its painted side shows. Glue or tape the coffee filter's edges together. Repeat with all the coffee filters.

6 String your bunting wherever you want to spread some holiday spirit!

FRUIT FLAG KEBABS

Skewer fruit into a snack that looks like the American flag!

WHAT YOU NEED

sharp knife
cutting board
strawberries
bananas
dinner knife
blueberries
wooden skewers
serving platter

14

1 Have an adult help you cut the stems off the strawberries. Then cut each strawberry in half the long way.

2 Peel the bananas. Cut them into pieces of equal size.

3 Slide seven blueberries onto one end of a skewer. Slide a banana onto the other end until it touches the blueberries.

4 Slide a strawberry on next to the banana. Slide on another banana, then another strawberry. Repeat until the skewer is full.

5 Repeat steps 3 and 4 with four skewers.

6 Build five skewers without blueberries. Put only strawberries and bananas on them.

7 Arrange the skewers to look like the US flag on the serving platter. Then, serve your patriotic snack to family and friends!

PRESIDENT PROFILE MEMORY GAME

Make a fun memory game with coins!

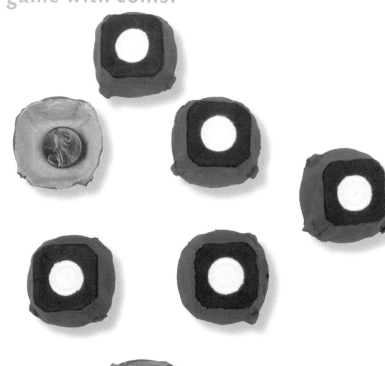

WHAT YOU NEED

cardboard egg carton

scissors

newspaper

acrylic paint

paintbrushes

hot glue gun & glue sticks

pairs of pennies, nickels, dimes & quarters

1 Cut eight cups off an egg carton.

2 Cover your work surface with newspaper. Paint all the cups to look exactly the same. Let the paint dry.

3 Place a dot of hot glue on the inside of one cup. Press a coin heads-up into the glue.

4 Repeat step 3 until you have made two cups for each type of coin.

5 Time to play! Place the cups upside down on a table. **Shuffle** them around.

6 Have player 1 flip a cup to reveal the coin. Have him or her flip a second cup. If the coins match, player 1 keeps the cups. If they do not match, player 1 flips both cups back over. Now it is player 2's turn.

7 Repeat step 6 until all the coins are matched. The player with the most president pairs wins!

STAR-SPANGLED WIND SOCK

Whip up a red, white, and blue wind sock to show your national pride!

WHAT YOU NEED

cardboard can

wooden skewer

newspaper

white & blue paint

paintbrushes

marker or pencil

cardboard

craft knife

cutting board

glitter glue

narrow ribbon

scissors

wide red ribbon

duct tape

1 Push the skewer all the way through the can near the bottom to make a set of holes. Remove the skewer.

2 Cover your work surface with newspaper. Paint the can blue. Let the paint dry.

3 Draw a star on cardboard. Have an adult help you cut out the star. This is a **stencil**.

4 Use the stencil to paint white stars on the can. Let the paint dry.

5 Outline the stars in glitter glue. Let the glue dry.

6 Cut a long piece of narrow ribbon. String it through the holes in the can. Tie the string's ends together to make a hanger.

7 Cut long strips of wide red ribbon. Tape one end of each inside the can. Then, hang your wind sock outside!

19

WASHINGTON'S TRICORN CAP

Make a hat that looks like the one the first president wore!

1 Measure the width of your forehead. Draw a hat shape as shown on a sheet of card stock. Make it 3 inches (8 cm) wider than the width of your forehead. Draw two pointed wings on each end of the shape.

2 Cut the shape out. This is your **template**.

3 Trace the template three times on blue paper. Cut all the shapes out.

4 Put glitter glue along the edges of the three hat pieces. Use short lines of glue spaced evenly apart. This is the hat's **stitching**. Let the glue dry.

(continued on next page)

TIP You can draw the hat stitching in marker instead of using glitter glue.

5 Fold the wings of each hat piece in toward the center. Press down on the folds. Unfold the wings.

6 Glue two hat pieces together. Put glue on the back of one wing. Line it up with the back of a wing on another hat piece. Press the wings together.

7 Glue the wings of the third hat piece to the other wings of the first and second hat pieces. This forms a triangle. Let the glue dry.

8 Decorate your **tricorn** hat with a button.

9 Punch a hole through the corner of the hat near the button.

10 Cut a piece of ribbon and thread it through the holes. Tie it in a bow. Wear your tricorn hat to dress up as President Washington!

8

9

10

PATRIOTIC WREATH

Display the colors of the US flag in a fun new way!

WHAT YOU NEED

large plate

marker or pencil

cardboard

scissors

paper in shades of red, white & blue

clear tape

craft glue

glitter

ribbon

1 Trace the plate on cardboard. Cut out the circle.

2 Roll a piece of colored paper into a cone as shown. Tape the cone together.

3 Repeat step 2 to make 15 to 20 cones in shades of red, white, and blue.

4 Glue the small ends of the cones around the cardboard circle. Let the glue dry.

5 Trace around the plate on blue paper. Cut out the circle. Draw a star inside it. Cover the star with glue and then glitter. Let the glue dry.

6 Glue the circle to the center of the wreath.

7 Cut a piece of ribbon. Tape its ends to the back of the wreath to make a hanger.

8 Hang your presidential decoration on a door to show your holiday spirit!

JEFFERSON'S WIG

Make a wig that looks like the powdered one
President Thomas Jefferson once wore!

WHAT YOU NEED

paper bag big
    enough to fit
    snugly on your
    head

marker

scissors

2 tall jars

cotton balls

craft glue

ribbon

1 Open the paper bag. Turn it upside down.

2 Draw a **hairline** around the bag. It should cross one narrow side near the top. Have the line curve downward on each wide side. Draw a **ponytail** on the other narrow side of the bag.

3 Cut the bag along the hairline and ponytail.

4 Put the bag over the two tall jars.

5 Glue cotton balls onto the bag. Cover its entire surface. Let the glue dry.

6 Cut a short piece of ribbon. Tie it in a bow. Glue the bow to the back of the wig, above the ponytail.

7 Wear your wig on Presidents' Day to look like President Jefferson!

LINCOLN'S LOG CABIN

President Lincoln lived in a log cabin as a boy. Build an edible version of his childhood home!

WHAT YOU NEED

cardboard

ruler

scissors

aluminum foil

newspaper

peanut butter

dinner knife

pretzel rods

graham crackers

shredded coconut

green food coloring

bowl

spoon

1. Cut out a square of cardboard that is 12 by 12 inches (30 by 30 cm). Cover it with aluminum foil. This is your base.

2. Cover your work surface with newspaper. Spread peanut butter along one side of two pretzel rods.

3. Set the two pretzel rods **parallel** to one another on the base. Space them 6 inches (15 cm) apart.

4. Place a dab of peanut butter near both ends of each pretzel rod.

5. Lay two more pretzel rods across the first two rods, on top of the peanut butter. The four pretzel rods should form a square.

(continued on next page)

6 Repeat steps 3 through 5 to build several layers of pretzel rod pairs. These are the cabin walls. Keep **stacking** pretzel rods until the cabin is as tall as you like.

7 Break three pretzel rods in half. Use a dinner knife to scrape one end of each piece into an angle. Scrape the other ends into flat surfaces.

8 Spread peanut butter on the angled ends of two pieces. Press the pieces together to form a peak. Repeat with the other pieces to create three pairs. These are the roof supports.

9 Cover the flat ends of each roof support with peanut butter. Place the roof supports in a row on top of the cabin.

10 Spread peanut butter on one side of a graham cracker. Stick it to the roof supports. Repeat with more graham crackers to complete the roof.

11 Slide two graham crackers under the pretzel rods and into the cabin. These make the cabin floor.

12 Spread peanut butter on the base around the cabin.

13 Stir several drops of green food coloring into a bowl of shredded coconut. This makes grass. Sprinkle it around the log cabin.

14 Set your little log cabin out during the holiday!

9

10

13

GLOSSARY ★

constitution – a written record of the basic beliefs and laws of a country that states the powers and duties of the government and the rights of the people.

hairline – the outline of a person's scalp hair, especially at the forehead.

parallel – lying or moving in the same direction but always the same distance apart.

ponytail – a hairstyle in which the hair is pulled together and banded, usually at the back of the head.

reenact – to put on a performance of a historical event, such as a battle.

Senate – one of the two houses of the US Congress that make laws.

shuffle – to rearrange to produce a random order.

stack – to put things on top of each other.

stencil – a flat piece of material with a cutout. It is used to trace or paint the cutout on another surface.

stitching – a row or line of thread left in fabric by moving the needle in and out.

template – a shape or pattern that is drawn or cut around to make the same shape in another material.

tradition – a belief or practice passed through a family or group of people.

tricorn – having three corners.